The SMALL and MIGHTY Book of Rainforests

Clive Gifford and Kirsti Davidson

Published in 2022 by OH!,
An imprint of Welbeck Children's Limited, part of Welbeck Publishing Group
Based in London and Sydney.

www.welbeckpublishing.com

Design and layout © Welbeck Children's Limited 2022
Text copyright © Welbeck Children's Limited 2022

All rights reserved. No part of this publication may be reproduced, stored in a retrieval system, or transmitted in any form or by any means, electronically, mechanical, photocopying, recording or otherwise, without the prior permission of the copyright owners and the publishers.

A CIP catalogue record for this book is available from the British Library.

Writer: Clive Gifford
Illustrator: Kirsti Davidson
Design and text by Raspberry Books Ltd
Project Manager: Russell Porter
Editorial Manager: Joff Brown
Design Manager: Matt Drew
Production: Jess Brisley

ISBN 978 1 83935 173 0

Printed in Heshan, China

10 9 8 7 6 5 4 3 2 1

FSC
www.fsc.org
MIX
Paper from responsible sources
FSC® C020056

The SMALL and MIGHTY Book of Rainforests

Clive Gifford and Kirsti Davidson

Contents

The World of Rainforests
9

Rainforest Plants
33

Creatures of the Rainforest
55

People and Rainforests **109**

Rainforest Record Breakers **131**

INTRODUCTION

This little book is full of facts about magnificent rainforests.

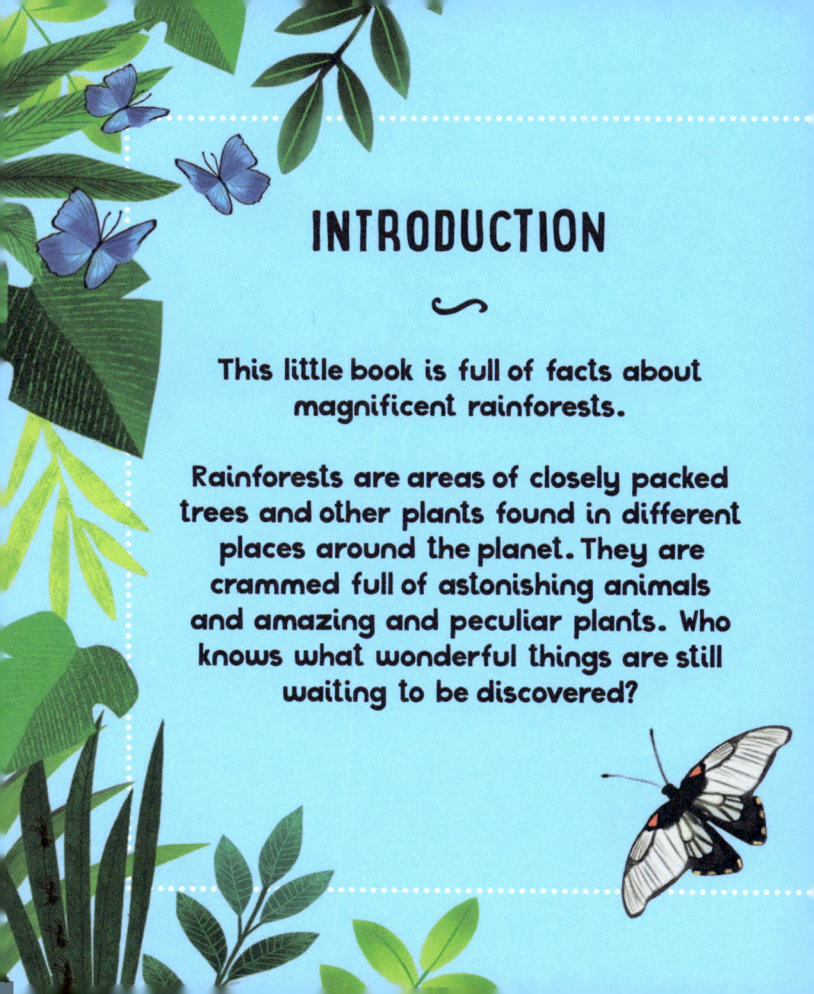

Rainforests are areas of closely packed trees and other plants found in different places around the planet. They are crammed full of astonishing animals and amazing and peculiar plants. Who knows what wonderful things are still waiting to be discovered?

You will find...

- 🌿 frogs with see-through bellies
- 🌿 plants that eat mice
- 🌿 a spider as big as your dinner plate

...and lots more.

Read on for an adventure through the world's most exciting habitat.

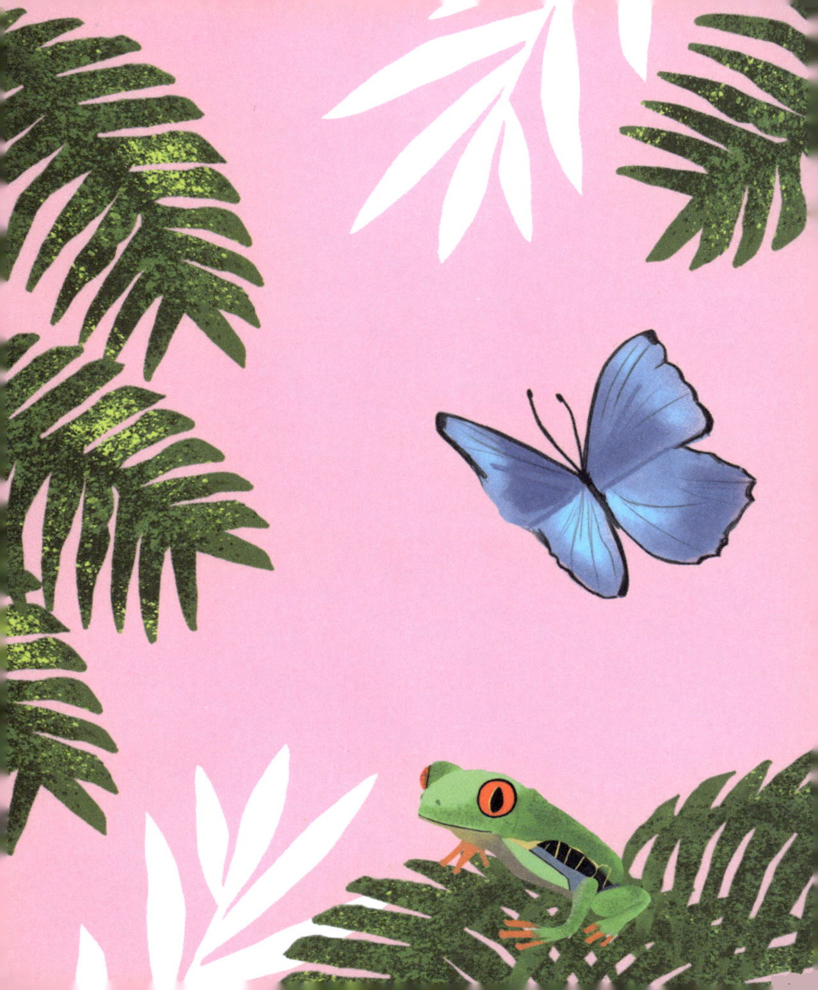

The World of Rainforests

Rainforests are found on **EVERY CONTINENT** except Antarctica. One of the most northerly is the Tongass rainforest, which is found in the United States' biggest protected forest area in Alaska.

The **TONGASS RAINFOREST** is a temperate rainforest, which means it is found in a part of the world that is not particularly hot or particularly cold.

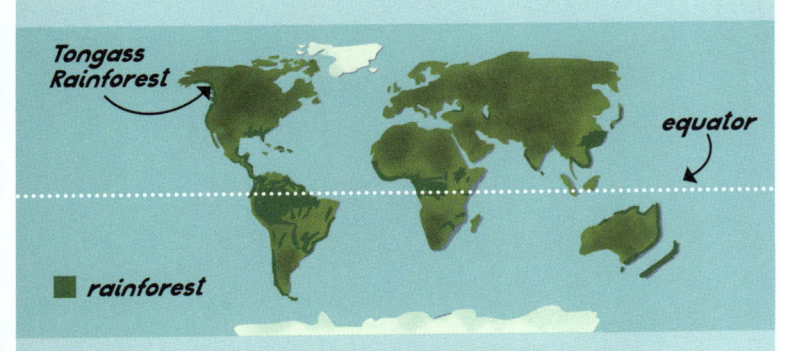

Tongass Rainforest

equator

■ *rainforest*

Tropical rainforests are found in warm parts of the world called the tropics. These are close to the **EQUATOR** – the imaginary line that runs around the middle of the Earth.

It is **NICE** and **WET** in the **RAINFOREST**. A tropical rainforest receives at least **200** cm of **RAINFALL** every **YEAR**. Some rainforests get drenched and receive five or six times that amount.

RAINFORESTS ARE HOME TO MORE THAN HALF OF ALL THE DIFFERENT KINDS OF PLANTS AND ANIMALS IN THE WORLD. BUT ALL THE RAINFORESTS ON EARTH WOULD FIT INTO THE COUNTRY OF BRAZIL ONE-AND-A-HALF TIMES.

THE AMAZON

is the world's largest rainforest.
It covers an area of over
5.5 million square km
– more than **22 times**
the size of the UK.

If it were a country, the Amazon rainforest would be the seventh **LARGEST** in the world.

The world's smallest tropical rainforest is found within a city. The Bukit Nanas Reserve in the Malaysian city of Kuala Lumpur has an area of just 0.1 square km but contains many trees as well as **MONKEYS** and **SNAKES**.

~ The ~
TALLEST trees in the rainforest can be **70** or **80 m** tall . . . and each releases about **760 litres** of water into the atmosphere each year – that's about **4 bathtubs of water!**

The **CANOPY** is a thick layer below the tallest trees. It is packed densely with plant life. The canopy blocks out so much sun that only a tiny amount of the sunlight that shines on the top of the rainforest reaches the forest floor below.

UNDERNEATH THE CANOPY

is the understorey. It's warm and damp down there and packed with insects, frogs, lizards and snakes.

Right at the bottom is the **forest floor**. It is dark here, and only about one-fifth of all the rain that falls on a rainforest ever reaches the forest floor.

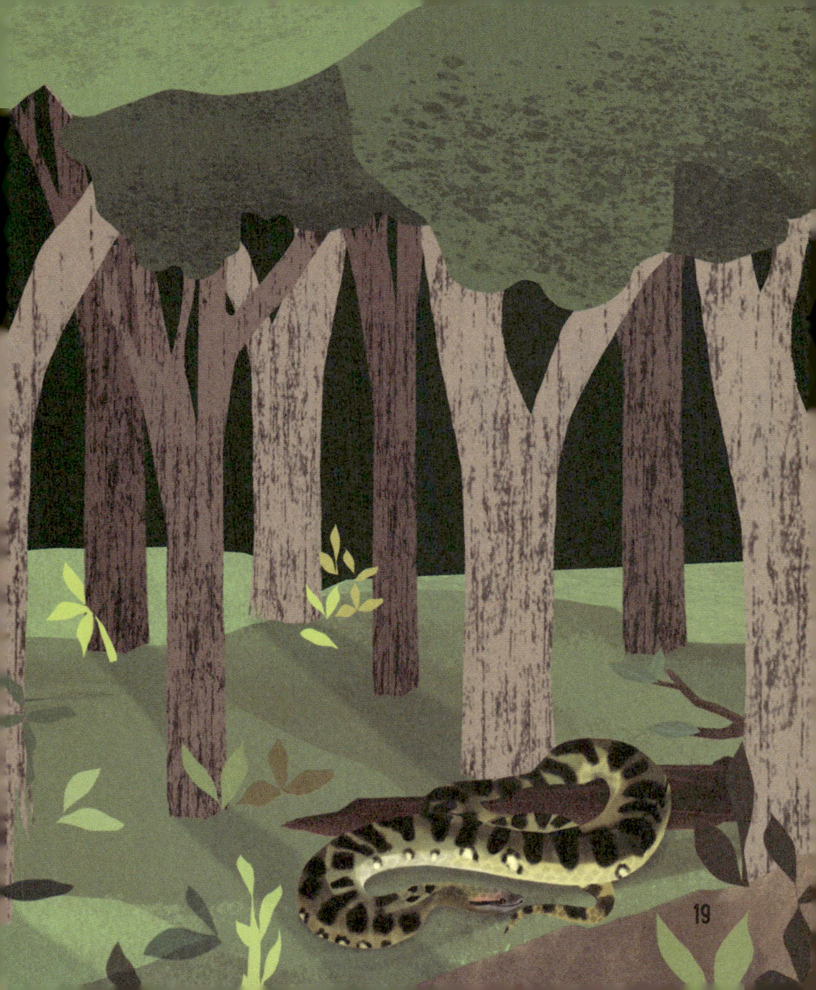

RAINFOREST TREES

Like all trees, rainforest trees absorb the gas **carbon dioxide** and store **carbon**. Carbon dioxide is one of the gases that are warming the world up and causing climate change. Because rainforests have so many millions of trees all storing carbon, they are very important in helping to **stop climate change.**

The Congo rainforest in central Africa absorbs about 1.2 billion tonnes of carbon dioxide every year.

That's about the weight of 10 million blue whales.

The **AMAZON RAINFOREST** covers parts of nine South American countries. Most of it is found in **Brazil**.

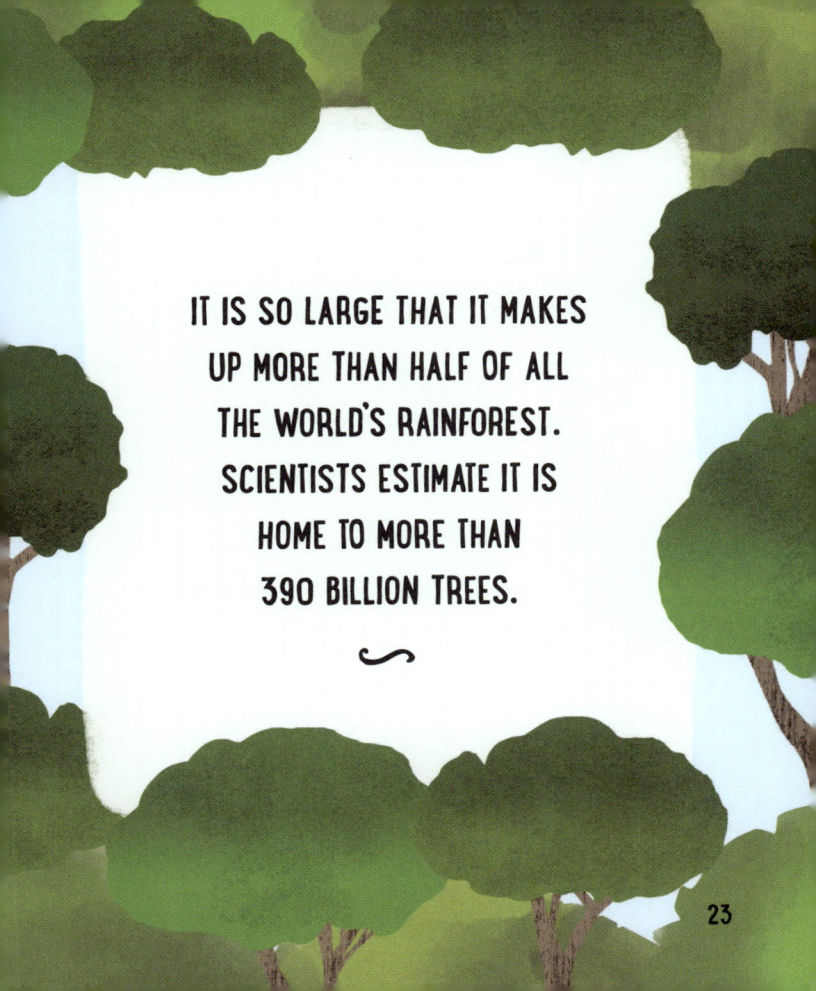

IT IS SO LARGE THAT IT MAKES UP MORE THAN HALF OF ALL THE WORLD'S RAINFOREST. SCIENTISTS ESTIMATE IT IS HOME TO MORE THAN 390 BILLION TREES.

Much of the **AMAZON RIVER** runs through rainforest. It's around 6,400 km long – about the distance between Rome in Italy and the US city of New York.

More than 1,100 other **rivers and large streams** all flow into the Amazon river. The river itself is home to more than **3,000 different species of fish.**

The
DAINTREE RAINFOREST
in north-eastern Australia is thought to be the oldest in the world. It formed **135 million years ago,** when dinosaurs still roamed the planet.

27

THE SINHARAJA FOREST

reserve in Sri Lanka is a protected area of rainforest about 88 square km in area. It is home to over 800 species of trees, animals including leopards, rare lizards, eagles and parrots, and is one of only a few places in the world where the **SRI LANKAN ELEPHANT** lives.

A rainforest on the Caribbean island of Dominica is home to **BOILING LAKE**, whose waters bubble away at piping hot temperatures of around 88 °C.

The lake is above a hole in the Earth's crust, and heat from molten magma (extremely hot liquid) beneath creates steam and hot gases.

SCIENTISTS THINK THERE'S
LOTS OF NEW RAINFOREST
LIFE STILL TO BE FOUND.

In 2020, a new GIANT frog,
15 species of wasps and a snake
were all discovered in rainforests
for the first time. The snake,
a pit viper, was named Salazar
after a wizard in Harry Potter
who could talk to snakes.

EXPEDITIONS to the Amazon rainforest between 2010 and 2013 DISCOVERED **441 NEW SPECIES.** These included **84 fish, 22 reptiles** and **18 birds** we didn't know of before.

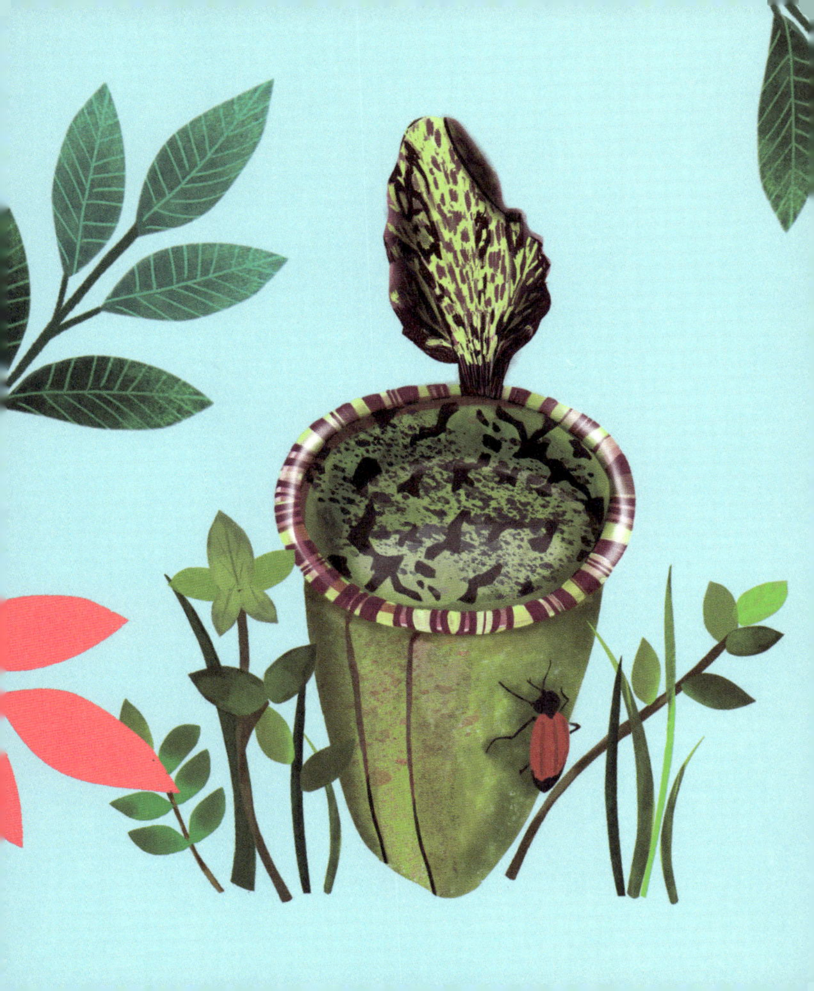

Rainforest Plants

WE GET LOTS OF USEFUL THINGS FROM RAINFOREST PLANTS. HERE ARE 10 OF THEM:

1. vanilla
2. coffee
3. pepper
4. paprika
5. pineapples
6. cashew nuts
7. cacao (used to make chocolate)
8. mangoes
9. bananas
10. sweet potatoes

The sap of the **HEVEA TREE**, originally found in South American rainforests, is collected to make natural rubber. The rubber is used in all sorts of products, from car tyres to footwear.

ORCHIDS

are beautiful flowering plants.
There are an amazing 20,000
known species of orchids
in tropical rainforests.

ORCHID SEEDS

are tiny and look like dust. A single orchid's seed pod can contain three million seeds.

STRANGLER FIGS

start as a seed landing on the branch of a tree. They grow downwards to the ground, smothering the tree and stealing some of its nutrients. There are two in Australia that are over 500 years old.

NOT ALL PLANTS NEED SOIL. Epiphytes are rainforest plants that cling to tall trees and other plants in the rainforest.

Found in the Amazon rainforest, the **GIANT WATER LILY** has 30-cm-wide flowers and giant, round, floating leaves that can spread up to 3 m wide.

The leaves are so strong
and float so well that you could
stand on one in the water
and it wouldn't sink.

SEVEN RAINFOREST PLANTS
with INTERESTING names:

1. Monkey face orchid
2. Hanging lobster claw
3. Monkey brush vine
4. Dancing girl ginger
5. Sausage tree
6. Flying duck orchid
7. Corpse flower

THE CORPSE FLOWER is a common name for either of two different plants, and both smell like rotten meat!

One is the **TITAN ARUM**, found in Asian rainforests. Its flowers only appear once every few years, when they open and stink out their surroundings

...JUST FOR 48 HOURS.

The other is called *RAFFLESIA ARNOLDII*. It is found in Asian rainforests and has no roots or leaves.

~ **ABOUT** ~
8 out of every 10
OF ALL THE FLOWERS
found in Australian rainforests
are not found anywhere
else in the world.

THE STINGING TREE

in Australia's Daintree rainforest is covered in tiny hairs coated with poisons. Touching this tree can give you a sting that is sore for many weeks.

THE BRAZIL NUT TREE

IS ONE OF THE TALLEST IN THE AMAZON RAINFOREST. THE SHELLS OF ITS NUTS ARE SO HARD THAT THEY CAN ONLY BE CRACKED OPEN BY TWO ANIMALS: THE MACAW (A TYPE OF PARROT) AND A BIG RODENT CALLED AN AGOUTI.

Jaguars

are meat-eating big cats, but some have been spotted eating whole avocados!

AZTEC ANTS

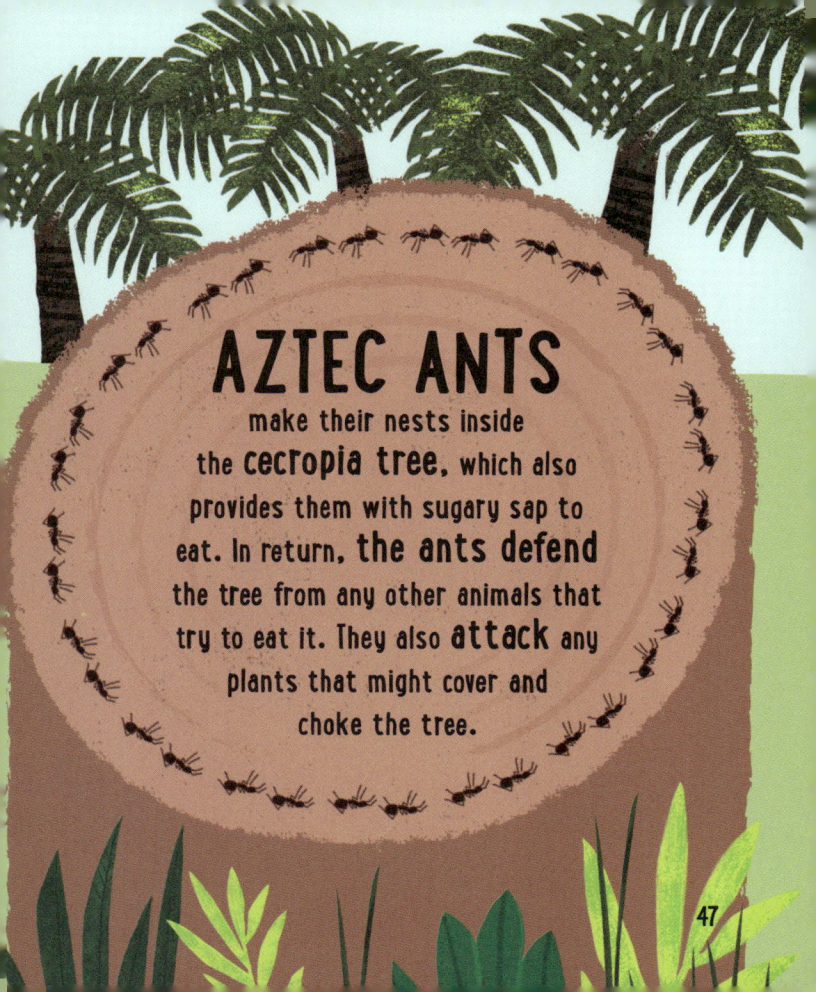

make their nests inside the **cecropia tree**, which also provides them with sugary sap to eat. In return, **the ants defend** the tree from any other animals that try to eat it. They also **attack** any plants that might cover and choke the tree.

TROPICAL PITCHER

plants eat flies and other insects that fall into the plant's long, **slippery traps** and cannot get out.

The largest tropical pitcher plant grows up to **1.5 m tall** and has tube-shaped traps that can even capture mice. It has been named **Attenborough's pitcher** plant after the famous naturalist Sir David Attenborough.

49

Sundew plants

have thin, hair-like tendrils tipped with sticky bits. Insects get stuck on these tendrils, and the leaf coils around the insect and takes up to six days to digest it.

If a small insect or tadpole touches a bladderwort plant, it's in

BIG TROUBLE.

The plant is covered in small pouches covered with a trapdoor that springs open and sucks the creature inside the plant to be eaten.

51

RAINFOREST PLANTS HAVE PROVIDED PEOPLE WITH ABOUT A QUARTER OF ALL THE MEDICINES WE USE. SCIENTISTS HAVE IDENTIFIED MORE THAN 2,000 TROPICAL RAINFOREST PLANTS THAT COULD BE USED TO TACKLE AND TREAT DIFFERENT TYPES OF CANCER.

THERE MAY BE MANY MORE HEALTH CURES LYING DEEP IN FORESTS. OUT OF ALL THE THOUSANDS OF RAINFOREST PLANTS THERE ARE IN THE WORLD, ONLY A FEW HAVE BEEN INVESTIGATED TO SEE IF THEY COULD BE USED IN MEDICINE.

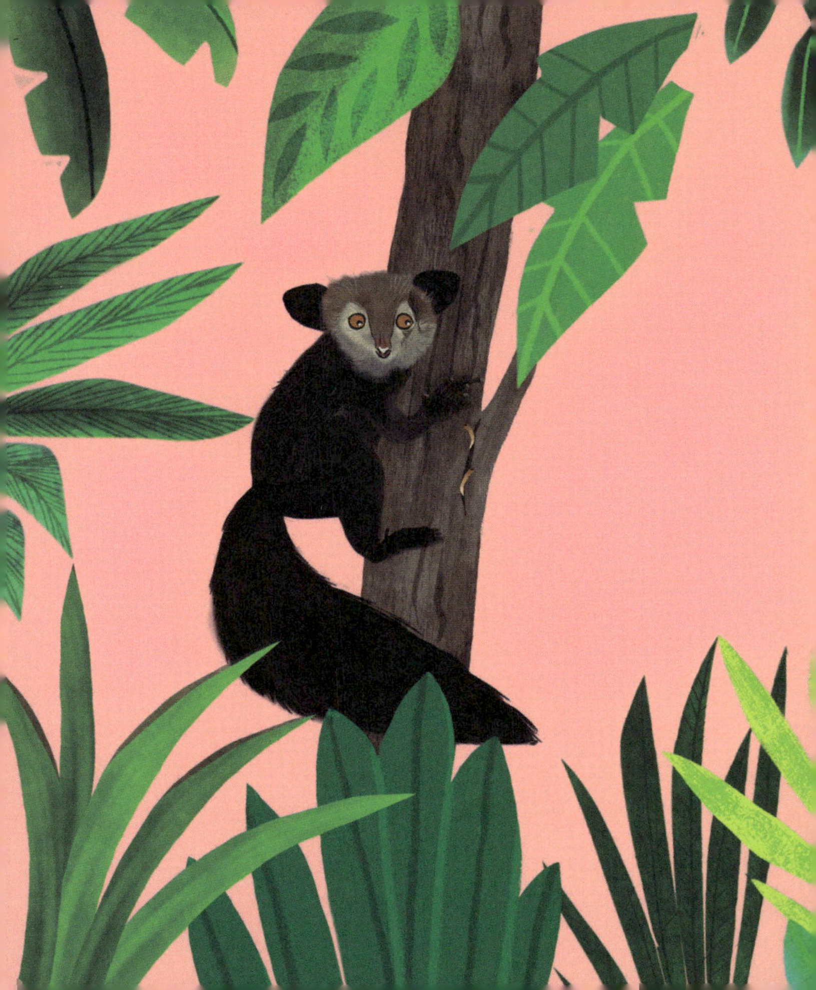

Creatures of the Rainforest

~ BLACK ~
HOWLER MONKEYS

make noisy neighbours.
They live in South American
rainforests and their calls can
be heard 5 km away.

Monkeys are just some of the
many different primates that live
in the world's rainforests.

Primates are a group of animals that includes
humans, apes, monkeys and some others.

12 RAINFOREST PRIMATES:

1. Woolly monkeys
2. Marmosets
3. Gibbons
4. Tamarins
5. Spider monkeys
6. Gorillas
7. Howler monkeys
8. Macaques
9. Slow lorises
10. Orangutans
11. Aye-ayes
12. Lemurs

THE AYE-AYE

is only found on the large island of Madagascar, off the coast of Africa. It spends all its life in the trees, prising insects and grubs out of tree trunks with its very long, bony middle fingers.

Male ring-tailed lemurs sometimes perform "STINK FIGHTS". They rub their tails in **SUPER SMELLY** substances secreted on their wrists and shoulders and wave their **STINKY TAILS** at each other. Such smelly battles for territory can last up to an hour. **PEW!**

ONE STRANGE SEE-THROUGH ANIMAL found in Central American rainforests is the glass frog. **It has a transparent belly,** which means you can spot its heart and other organs inside.

blue jeans frog

10 tropical rainforest frogs:

1. Strawberry poison dart frog
2. Blue jeans frog
3. Red-eyed tree frog
4. Mimic poison frog
5. Black-legged dart frog
6. Glass frog
7. Pinocchio frog
8. Tomato frog
9. Amazon horned rain frog
10. Striped rocket frog

Found in the
Congo rainforest,
OKAPIS are related to
GIRAFFES,
but their
STRIPED SKIN
makes them look
a little like ZEBRAS.

Their oily fur is waterproof – handy when you live somewhere that gets so much rain.

～ Okapis ～

have 35-cm-long tongues – long enough to lick their own ears and eyelids! They grip leaves and branches with their tongues and pull them into their mouths.

Giant columns of
ARMY ANTS

march around the rainforest floor in some places. They have large claws and a powerful sting. Working together, they can catch and gobble up lizards and other creatures much larger than themselves.

As insects flee the terrifying columns of army ants, sneaky creatures like robber flies and antbirds lurk, ready to pounce and gobble the insects up.

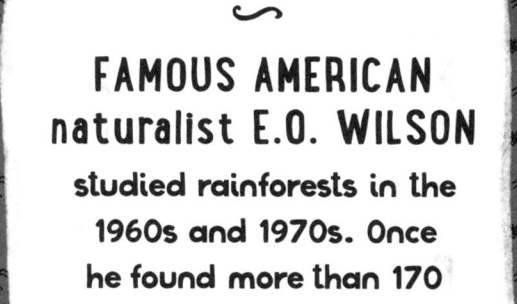

FAMOUS AMERICAN naturalist E.O. WILSON studied rainforests in the 1960s and 1970s. Once he found more than 170 different species of ant living in a small plot of rainforest trees in New Guinea.

THE HONDURAN
~ WHITE BAT ~

is fluffy and white with a
yellow mouth and nose. It is found
in Central American rainforests,
where it lives inside little tents it
makes out of leaves.

Three-toed sloths sleep upside down, hanging from a branch. They **snooze** for as long as 15 hours a day – what **lazybones!**

～ The ～
BIGGEST show-offs

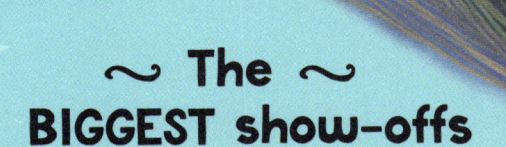

in the rainforests of Papua New Guinea must
be male blue birds of paradise. To impress
females, they fan out their dazzling tail feathers
and hang upside down from branches.

SIX
BIRDS OF PARADISE WITH GREAT NAMES!

1. Twelve-wired bird of paradise
2. Magnificent riflebird
3. Obi paradise crow
4. Trumpet manucode
5. Growling riflebird
6. Superb bird of paradise

A GIANT ANTEATER

has no teeth but an amazing tongue that grows up to 60 cm long. The tongue can be flicked in and out of the creature's mouth up to 160 times a minute.

An adult giant anteater uses its **BIG FRONT CLAWS** to dig up ant or termite nests. Using its **AMAZING TONGUE**, it can eat up to 30,000 ants a day!

There may be 2.5 million different species of insect in the Amazon rainforest – scientists haven't discovered and counted them all up yet!

There are
1,300 different species of butterfly
found in the rainforests of Peru's Manú National Park. That's nearly twice the number found in the entire United States.

IF YOU'RE SCARED of SPIDERS,

the Amazon rainforest may not be the best place for you.
At least 3,600 different species of spider live there!

In the Amazon, **jumping** spiders can leap 50 times their own body length in a single bound. If you had that ability, you could jump **60 to 80 m!**

∽

Ancylometes spiders live in rainforests in Central and South America. They can spin silky webs above and in water and even dive underwater to catch insects, small lizards and baby fish.

GREEN ANACONDAS

are enormous snakes that grow to at least 5 m long and can weigh 70 kg – as much as an adult man.

They coil themselves around their prey and then swallow it whole without chewing.

There are more than 60 different species of piranha fish. The red-bellied piranha has a powerful bite and triangle-shaped, razor-sharp teeth. It gets a large part of its diet from fins that it nips off the tails of other fish.

The **ELECTRIC EEL** is one powerful Amazon fish. Special cells in its body allow it to deliver a 600-volt electric shock to stun fish, birds and small mammals, when it is hunting, or to defend itself from predators.

Meet the lizard
THAT CAN WALK ON WATER!
If it's attacked, the common basilisk can run on its two back legs across the surface of a pool or pond to escape. It lives in rainforests in Central and South America.

The **HARPY EAGLE**'s 13-cm-long claws are longer than a **grizzly bear**'s. It uses them to grab **monkeys**, **sloths** and **parrots** from the **treetops** of the Amazon rainforest.

THE MARGAY

is a wild cat found in rainforests in Central and South America. It has learned to mimic the cries of a baby tamarin monkey. This lures adult monkeys towards the margay for the cat to catch and eat.

The Caquetá titi monkey lives in the Amazon rainforest. When baby Caquetá titi monkeys are happy, they **purr** just like **cats**!

A male **PROBOSCIS MONKEY'S NOSE** can grow up to 17 cm long, making it a quarter of his total head and body length.

Beware the **GOLDEN POISON DART FROG.** Although it's only the length of a paperclip, this small frog carries enough poison on its skin to kill 10 adult humans.

Male **STRAWBERRY POISON DART FROGS** will wrestle each other for 20 minutes at a time. Their bouts take place in Central American rainforests.

To startle predators and
gain time to escape,
THE RED-EYED TREE FROG
opens its red eyes wide and waves
its bright orange feet!

∽ The ∽
pygmy marmoset
is a tiny monkey, but it's
very bouncy! It can jump
5 m high as it springs
through the trees in the
Amazon rainforest.

GIBBONS live in the rainforests of Southeast Asia. They swing from tree to tree at **amazing speeds –** up to **50 km/h**. That's faster than you can pedal your bike!

THE GOLDEN LION TAMARIN of Brazil's Atlantic rainforest keeps moving and sleeps in different places, mostly holes in trees. This is so its scent doesn't build up in one place, which would attract predators.

Dozens of species of **hummingbirds** live in South and Central American rainforests. They beat their wings very fast – up to 70 or 80 times a second. They're the only type of bird that can fly forwards and backwards and even hover in mid-air.

Almost half the length of a
TOCO TOUCAN
is its giant bill. It uses the bill to pluck juicy fruit from plants and occasionally snap up insects or the eggs of other birds.

~ Jaguars ~

roam the rainforests of South and Central America.

A jaguar's bite is more powerful than a lion's. Deer, sloths, turtles, monkeys and even crocodiles are on their menu.

VISAYAN WARTY PIGS

are only found in rainforests in the Philippines. They are not fussy eaters, scoffing palms, wild bananas, earthworms, mice and rats. Male warty pigs can grow up to four times the size of females.

The three-toed SLOTH creeps along v-e-r-y s-l-o-w-l-y...

. . . most people can walk **20 times faster** than this slow-moving creature crawls. Algae, beetles and moths all make a home in its fur.

∽

The sloth only goes for a **poo once a week.** It slowly climbs down from its tree branch and digs a toilet with its claws.

Orangutans

are found only in the rainforests of Southeast Asia. They are amazingly agile and swing from tree to tree using their arms, which are one-and-a-half times as long as their legs.

Orangutans **BUILD A NEW PLACE TO SLEEP** in the treetops every night, weaving together tree branches to make a supportive mattress.

95

A type
of possum called a
SUGAR GLIDER
can glide 50 m between treetops in rainforests in Indonesia, Papua New Guinea and Australia. It has sheets of skin joining its wrists to its ankles. When it holds its legs out, the skin

s t r e t c h e s

out like wings and it glides
through the air.

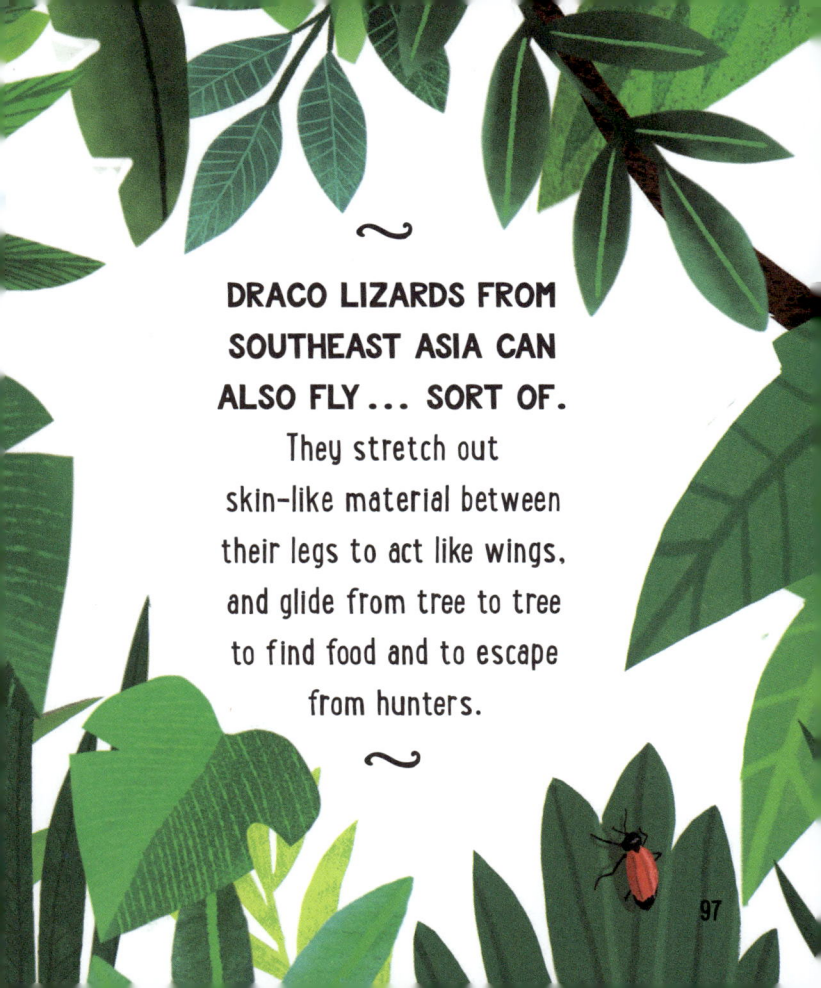

DRACO LIZARDS FROM SOUTHEAST ASIA CAN ALSO FLY... SORT OF.

They stretch out skin-like material between their legs to act like wings, and glide from tree to tree to find food and to escape from hunters.

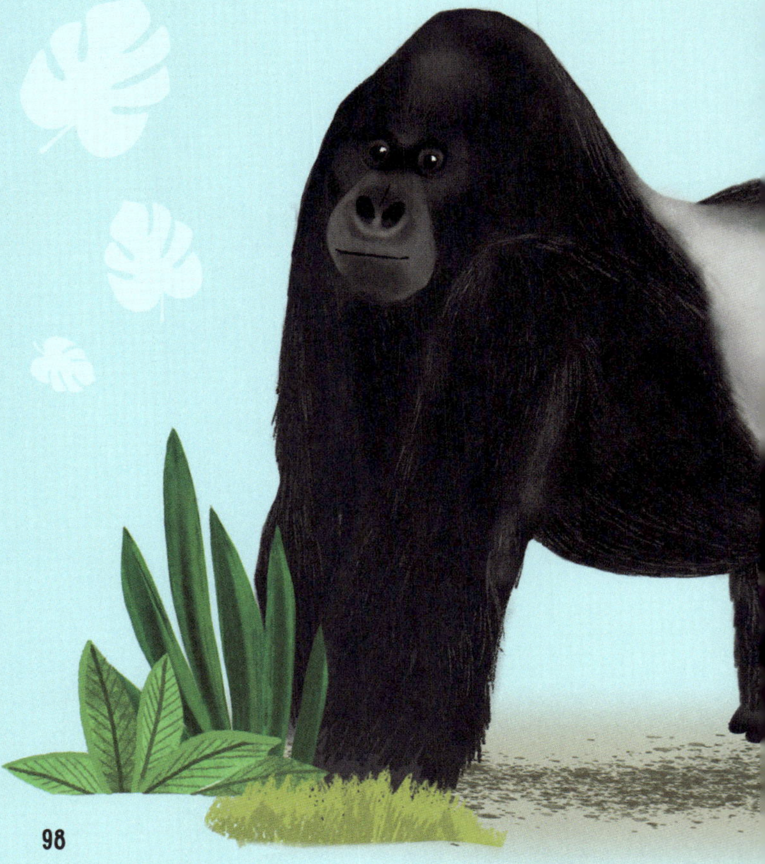

There are only
~ 1,000 or so ~
# MOUNTAIN GORILLAS
left in the wild,
all living in dense
rainforest in central Africa.

A mountain gorilla eats
as much as 30 kg of
plants and berries a day.

A male mountain gorilla can weigh over 200 kg,
about the weight of three adult humans.

Most dolphins are found in the oceans,

but the pink river dolphin lives in the rivers of the Amazon rainforest. It performs gymnastic moves in the water. It eats crabs, turtles and fish, including fearsome piranhas!

The pink river dolphin can be curious and playful. Its brain is almost one-and-a-half times bigger than ours.

Four PINK rainforest animals:

ROSEATE SKIMMER
- a bright pink dragonfly that lives in ponds and swamps in parts of Brazil

PINK LEAF BEETLE
- a shocking pink beetle found in the jungles of Peru

ORCHID MANTIS

- an insect found in Indonesia that tricks flies into thinking it's a flower by crouching on top of plants

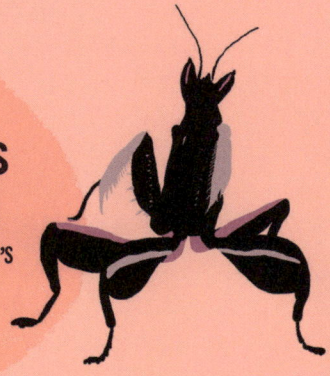

PHILTRONOMA CBDORA

- a butterfly from Costa Rica, discovered in 2019, that has two pink wings and two grey wings

BEAUTIFUL BUT DEADLY,

the Bengal tiger may walk up to 19 km a night. It moves silently on its soft paw pads as it stalks large prey. It lives in rainforests in India and neighbouring countries.

THE BENGAL TIGER

can live off one

LARGE MEAL

a week.

Imagine a GUINEA PIG that weighs as much as your teacher!

The **CAPYBARA** is the world's biggest rodent and a close relative of the guinea pig.

The LARGEST capybaras weigh 60-70 kg and eat up to 4 kg of grass and water plants every day. That's about the weight of 16 sandwiches.

Despite their bulk, capybaras are skilled swimmers and can hold their breath underwater for five minutes at a time to hide from predators.

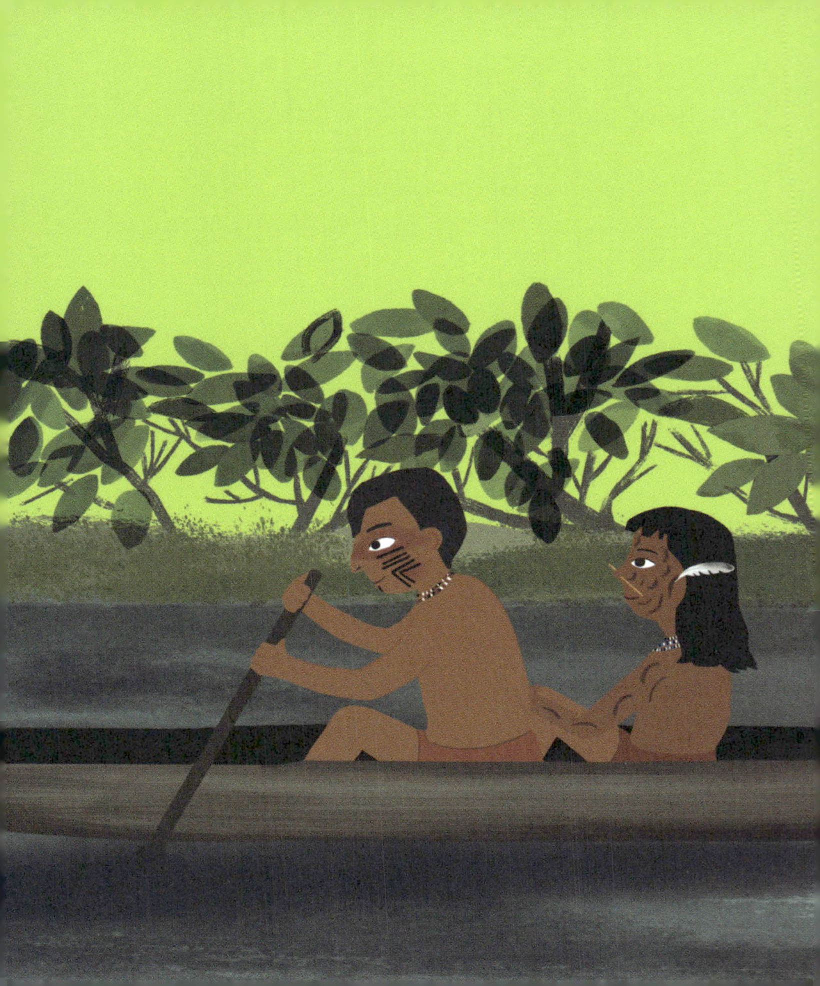

People and Rainforests

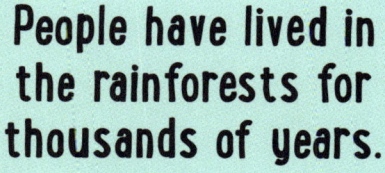

People have lived in the rainforests for thousands of years.

There are thought to be as many as

50 million people

living in rainforests today.
Many farm in small clearings,
gather food from the forest
or guide tourists.

A small number of rainforest people live in out-of-the-way parts of big rainforests.

SOME HAVE NEVER, EVER MADE CONTACT WITH THE MODERN WORLD.

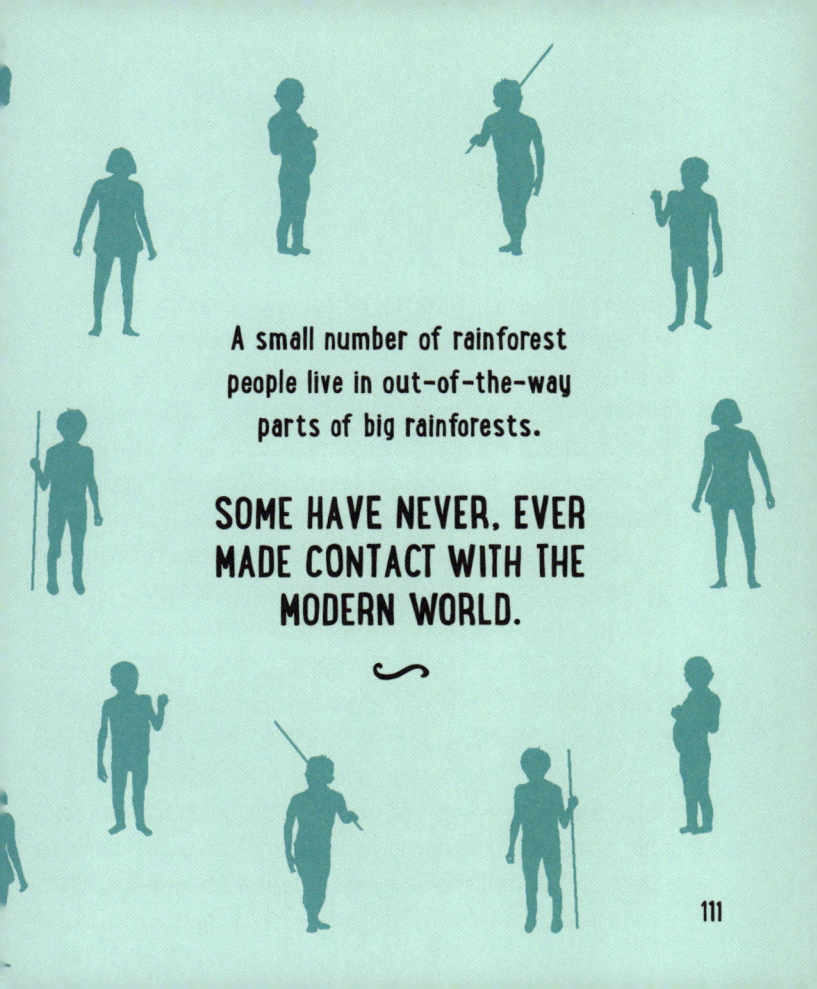

Around 35,000 YANOMANI people live in the Amazon rainforest.

They grow crops in small clearings and sometimes hunt **deer** and **monkeys** using bows and arrows.

The **Korowai people** live in the rainforests of Papua New Guinea in tree houses. Some of the houses are as high as 20–40 m above the ground.

The **Mbuti people** live in Africa's Ituri rainforest. They get their food from all levels of the rainforest – from gathering berries on the forest floor to setting traps for birds high in the treetops.

People have always used items from rainforests, even if they didn't live there. More than 1,000 years ago, the ancient Chinese filled sections of bamboo with **GUNPOWDER** to create the world's **FIRST ROCKETS** and **FIREWORKS**.

BAMBOO IS USED FOR LESS EXPLOSIVE PURPOSES TODAY, INCLUDING SCAFFOLDING AROUND TALL BUILDINGS AND CLOTHING THAT IS MADE FROM SHREDDED BAMBOO TURNED INTO FIBRES.

In 1799–1800, epic explorers **ALEXANDER VON HUMBOLDT** AND **AIMÉ BONPLAND** TRAVELLED THROUGH OVER 2,700 KM OF SOUTH AMERICAN RAINFOREST, **DISCOVERING 6,000 CREATURES** THAT EUROPEANS HAD NEVER SEEN BEFORE.

In the early 1890s, **Mary Kingsley** explored some of Africa's rainforests on her own, spending time with local people and studying the animals. On her adventures she always wore heavy wool skirts and carried an umbrella, dressing like she might have done at home in England. The umbrella came in handy for prodding hippos away.

IN 2012,
explorer and conservationist
JULIAN BAYLISS
discovered a complete rainforest hidden in the cone of a long-dead volcano, Mount Lico, in the African nation of Mozambique. He first spotted the forest when studying aerial photographs and got to visit it and film the forest five years later.

IN 2007,
MARTIN STREL
– A SWIMMER FROM SLOVENIA – SWAM MOST OF THE LENGTH OF THE AMAZON RIVER. HIS 5,265 KM-LONG SWIM TOOK 66 DAYS.

More than half the world's rainforests have been LOST in the last 100 years.

Some rainforest trees have been **CUT DOWN** for their wood. Far more have been **DESTROYED** to clear land for farm fields or for grazing farm animals such as cattle.

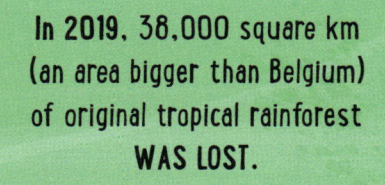

In 2019, 38,000 square km (an area bigger than Belgium) of original tropical rainforest **WAS LOST.**

Every year for the past **10 years,** roughly a **soccer pitch's** worth of rainforest has been **DESTROYED** every six seconds.

Disappearing
rainforests mean disappearing homes for many creatures.

The number of woolly monkeys has halved in the last 50 years, mainly due to their homes being destroyed.

On the island of Borneo,
half of the forests where orangutans live
have been **chopped down** or **burned** in the past
25 years. As a result, the number of
orangutans has dropped by almost half.

～ The ～
Sumatran rhino

once roamed forested parts of India, Thailand and Malaysia. There are now fewer than 100 left in the wild, all in Indonesia.

Costa Rica lost **MORE THAN A THIRD** of its rainforests in 40 years. Thankfully, action was taken.

Trees were replanted and farmers began to farm land without cutting down any more rainforest. As a result, nearly two-thirds of the country is now covered in forest.

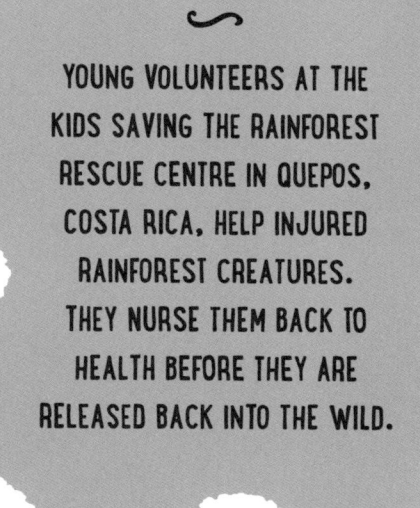

YOUNG VOLUNTEERS AT THE KIDS SAVING THE RAINFOREST RESCUE CENTRE IN QUEPOS, COSTA RICA, HELP INJURED RAINFOREST CREATURES. THEY NURSE THEM BACK TO HEALTH BEFORE THEY ARE RELEASED BACK INTO THE WILD.

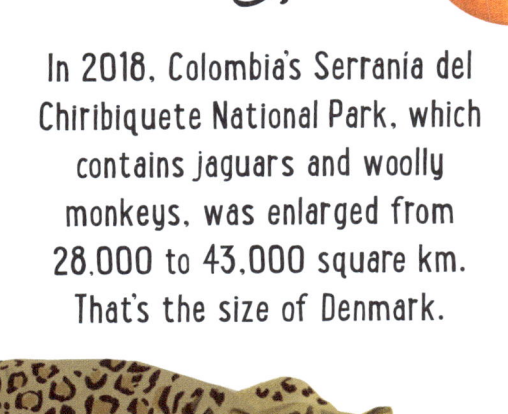

In 2018, Colombia's Serranía del Chiribiquete National Park, which contains jaguars and woolly monkeys, was enlarged from 28,000 to 43,000 square km. That's the size of Denmark.

In 2020, the **Rainforest Trust charity** raised enough money to protect a part of the Choco rainforest in Colombia, which is home to creatures like the **golden poison dart frog.**

∽

There are plans to expand the Sinharaja rainforest reserve in Sri Lanka to make it four times bigger than it is now. **This will help protect more rare species of plants and animals.**

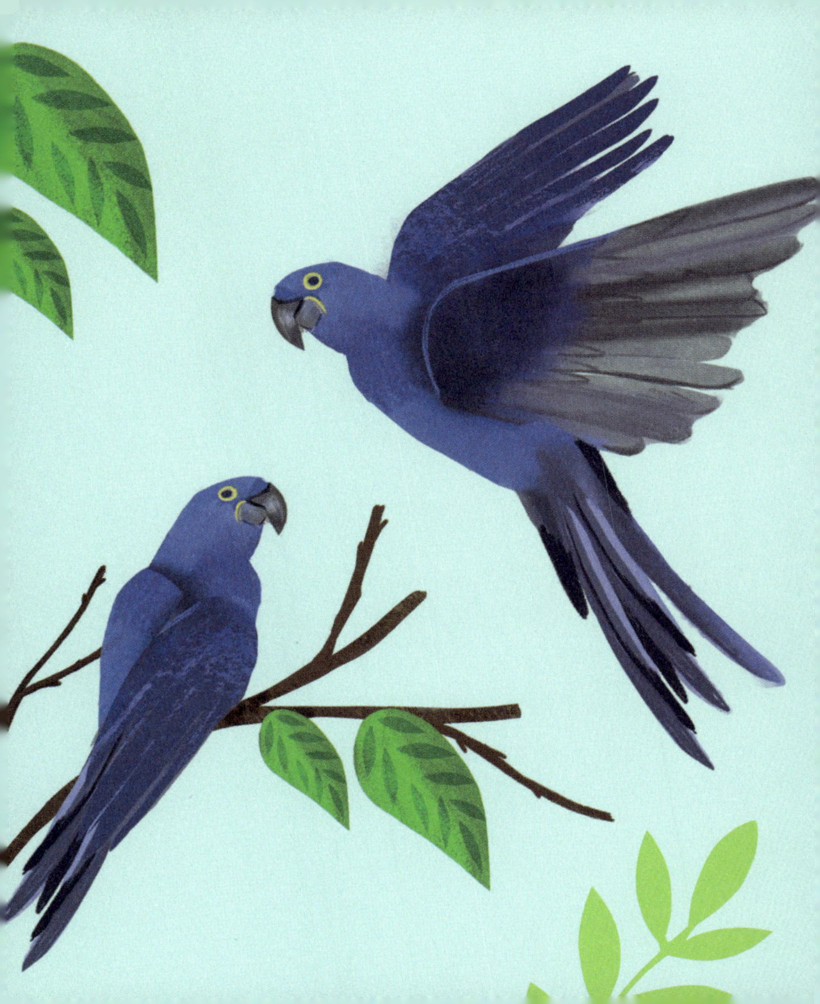

Rainforest Record Breakers

THE FIRST PERSON TO WALK ALL THE WAY ALONG THE LENGTH OF THE AMAZON RIVER WAS EDWARD STAFFORD FROM THE UK...

THE AMAZON RIVER is not the longest in the world (the Nile is), but it holds the most water of any river in the world.

...WHO TOOK 2 YEARS, 4 MONTHS AND 8 DAYS TO WALK IT.

THE EASTERN GORILLA is the world's **HEAVIEST** ape, weighing up to 267 kg. It lives in African rainforests.

The pygmy marmoset

is the world's smallest monkey. It grows up to 14 cm long and weighs 90 g – half the weight of a hamster. It lives in South American rainforests.

The **LARGEST** flower in the world is the *RAFFLESIA ARNOLDII*, found in Indonesian rainforests. Each bloom can measure up to 107 cm across and weigh up to 11 kg. That's heavier than two pet cats.

Rafflesia arnoldii

Titan arum

Other names for *Rafflesia arnoldii* include the **MONSTER** flower and the **CORPSE** flower. It is **VERY smelly**, but the other corpse flower, the Titan arum, is officially the smelliest plant.

THE WORLD'S FASTEST-GROWING PLANT is the bamboo. There are over 1,000 different kinds of bamboo plant found in rainforests. Many grow as fast as 91 cm in a single day.

The DURIAN tree, which grows in Southeast Asian rainforests, produces the world's smelliest fruits. They stink so much that you are not allowed to carry them on buses and trains in some countries.

The **HOATZIN** holds the record for the **smelliest bird** in the world. The Amazon rainforest bird has insides similar to a cow's, good for digesting leaves. It **SMELLS** like **COW MANURE**.

THE HYACINTH MACAW

is the largest flying parrot in the world, with a wingspan of up to 127 cm. That's almost as wide as you are tall!

∽ The ∽
BIGGEST BIRD
in any rainforest
is the Philippine eagle.
It has a wingspan of up
to 220 cm and weighs
more than 6 kg.

In 2011, **PROFESSOR CHRIS AUSTIN** discovered the world's smallest frog species living on the rainforest floor at Amau in Papua New Guinea. The frog measures just 7.7 mm long. That's less than the size of your thumbnail!

The world's **LARGEST** butterfly is the Queen Alexandra's birdwing, which is found in just one rainforest in Papua New Guinea. Females grow much larger than males – the largest can have a wingspan of 28 cm.

The **BIGGEST** and **HEAVIEST** rainforest **SPIDER** is the fearsome **GOLIATH BIRDEATER.** Weighing up to 170 g and with a leg span of 28 cm, it's the size of a dinner plate. Despite the name, these spiders rarely eat birds, and mostly eat **insects, earthworms** and **small lizards.**